THE ULTIMATE UNDERWEAR JOKEBOOK

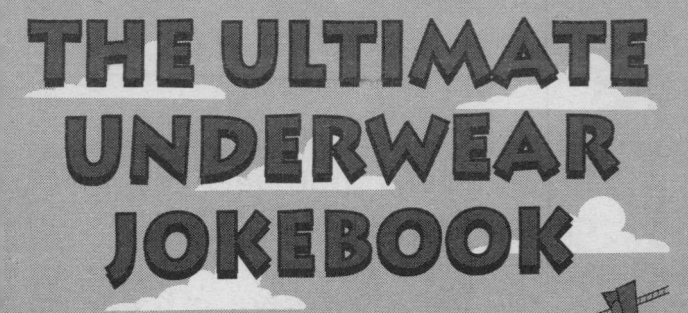

by Chris Tait

kidsbooks
Incorporated

Copyright © 2002 Kidsbooks, Inc.
230 Fifth Avenue
New York, NY 10001

Manufactured in Canada

Visit us at www.kidsbooks.com
Volume discounts availabl

W9-CQU-623

What did the boxer shorts say to the socks that were drying on the line?

You hang out here often?

What kind of underwear works best for small dogs?

Boxer shorts, of course!

Knock, knock!
Who's there?
Lucy!
Lucy who?
Lucy lastic will make your underwear fall down!

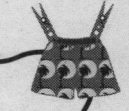

What did the man say when he took off his too-tight underwear?

That's a brief relief!

Did you read the book about the history of underwear?

Yes, but I thought it was a little brief!

What do you call your evening underwear?

Late bloomers!

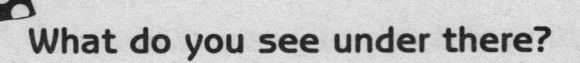

What do you see under there?

Underwear?

What do you call instructions
for underwear?

The brief brief!

Why do underwear hate these
kinds of books?

*Because they're always the
butt of the joke!*

Words of wisdom: Don't wear polka-dot underwear under white shorts.

≋

What part of the military handles the underwear?

The rear admiralty!

≋

Knock, knock!
Who's there?
Nunya!
Nunya who?
Nunya business what kind of boxer shorts I'm wearing!

≋

How did the boxer feel when he ran out of underpants?

Short-tempered!

What advice do you give to a contortionist about his underwear?

Don't get your shorts in a knot!

If superheroes are so smart, why do they wear their underpants over their pants?

What did the man call the full-body underwear that he lost?

His long-gones!

How can your friends help you with your underwear in a pinch?

With a wedgie!

What do you call a man
who forgets to put on his
underpants?

Nicholas! (knicker-less)

≈

Knock, knock!
Who's there?
Irish.
Irish who?
*Irish my underwear
wasn't showing!*

≈

What did the pair of
underwear say when he was
making a toast?

Bottoms up!

What did the man say when he took out his thermal underwear for the winter?

Long time, no seam!

What did the woman do with her silky underwear?

She satin them!

What kind of boxer shorts do supervillains wear?

Underworld underwear!

Why are boxer shorts so sad?

Because they feel under appreciated!

What did the army shorts say to the boxer shorts?

Brief me!

What do you feel when you have to throw out an old pair of underwear?

Brief grief!

What kind of briefs do cows wear?

Udderwear!

≈

What kind of briefs does Thor wear?

Thunderpants!

Why was the musician so embarrassed when his shorts fell down?

Because he thought the band had let him down!

What did the tank top say to the pair of long underwear?

Let's keep this brief!

What did the long underwear say to the tank top?

Don't be short with me!

What kind of dessert can you
eat in your underwear?

Shortbread!

What did the silk underwear
say to the cotton briefs?

**Slip around, you might
learn something!**

What did the cotton briefs say
to the silk underwear?

Man, you're smooth!

What do you call a telephone receptionist who wears silk boxer shorts?

A smooth operator!

What kind of underwear do sheep wear?

Baaaaaxer shorts!

What do elephants wear to the beach?

Their swim trunks!

What do you call bleached briefs that shrink in the wash?

Whitey tighties!

≋

Knock, Knock!
Who's there?
Ican!
Ican who?
Ican see your underwear!

≋

What kind of underwear do gardeners wear?

Bloomers!

≋

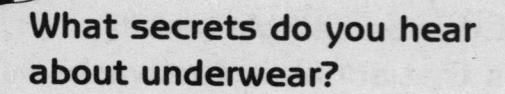

What secrets do you hear about underwear?

Bloomer rumors!

What do you call scratchy woolen underwear?

Itchy britchies!

Why did Santa need new underwear?

Because his were full of ho-ho-holes!

What famous bear needs to wear diapers?

Winnie the Pooh!

What do you call someone who steals underwear from babies?

A diaper swiper!

What do you call a bucket where you keep old baby underwear?

The Pampers hamper!

What did the sign over the underwear store say?

Get your butt in here!

What does someone who
makes underwear do?

He stitches britches!

What did the nice woman say
to the man in his swimming
trunks?

Those really suit you!

What did the vacationer say
when he got too much sand in
his swimsuit?

*I think I overpacked my
trunks!*

What do you call the money
you use to buy underwear?

Shortbread!

What kind of underwear does
Muhammed Ali wear?

Boxers, of course!

What kind of swimsuits do
pelicans wear?

Beak-inies!

What did the swimmer say
about the little bikini?

It was itsy-bitsy teenie-weenie!

How did the woman in the
full-bodied swimsuit feel after
escaping a shark?

**She felt lucky to be
in one piece!**

What is the fastest swimsuit around?

The Speedo!

What did the sunbather have after falling asleep in his Speedo?

Hot crossed buns!

Why did the fast swimmer have to pull out of the race?

He got pulled over for Speedo-ing!

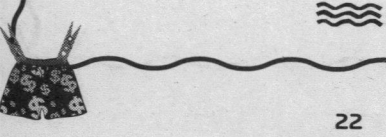

What did the woman call her fun, fancy underwear?

Her silly frillies!

What kind of underwear do baseball players wear?

Short stops!

Knock, knock!
Who's there?
C-2!
C-2 who?
C-2 it that you don't forget to wear your underwear!

What do you call old
underwear?

Behind the times!

What kind of underwear do
New York basketball players
like to wear?

Knick-ers!

What do you call a baby snake that wears diapers?

> *A diaper viper!*

Why won't Ron wear white underwear?

> *Because you can't white a Ron!*

Where do you keep your shorts when you travel?

> *In your briefcase!*

What kind of underwear do horses wear?

> *Jockeys!*

What kind of jumps do jockeys do?

> *Girdle hurdles!*

≈≈≈

Why did the woman keep checking her pantyhose drawer?

> *Because she needed to take stocking!*

≈≈≈

What do you call it when
Santa checks his inventory?

Christmas stocking!

What kind of underwear do
comedians wear?

Joke-ys!

What kind of socks do
firefighters wear?

Fire hose!

What kind of socks do horn
players wear?

Tuba socks!

≋

Why did the underwear keep
moving around?

*Because it was jockeying for
position!*

≋

Knock, knock!
Who's there?
Handel!
Handel who?
*Handel your underwear
with care!*

What did the boxer shorts say to the pantyhose?

Sock it to me!

What kind of underwear fits over a shell?

A turtle girdle!

What kind of shirt do generals wear under their suits?

Tank tops, of course!

Where do pantyhose go to meet stockings?

To a sock hop!

How do you cover up your foot?

You socket!

≋

What do chickens wear under their pants?

Hen-derwear!

Why do stockings always feel safe?

Because they've got a garter!

What do you call a shirt that Sir Lancelot wears to sleep?

A knight shirt!

Knock, knock!
Who's there?
Warren!
Warren who?
I'm Warren my favorite pair of underwear!

What is a pair of stockings'
favorite sports team?

*The Boston Red Socks,
of course!*

What are the best initials for
comfy sleeping?

P.J.!

What do you call bright
yellow PJs?

Banana pajamas!

What do you call indoor shoes that help you slide?

House slippers!

What do you call PJs that are too small?

Tighty nighties!

What kind of underwear does a home wear?

A house coat!

What do you call shoes that you wear to bed?

Sleeper slippers!

What do you call a house-coat that you wear to make a salad?

A dressing gown!

What do you call women's shorts that are always behind?

Fanny!

What does the green-thumbed woman wear under her shoes?

Garden hose!

What does the postman wear on his feet at night?

Shipper slippers!

What do you call it when you throw out the top of your underwear?

Waist-band!

What do underwear like to read?

Boxer short stories!

What do you call it when you quickly alter your long underwear?

A short cut!

What's a good nickname for little underwear?

Short stuff!

What do you call it when a baby wets its diaper?

Britches over troubled water!

What advice did the
underwear give the man?

Don't wear me out!

Knock, knock!
Who's there?
Tom Sawyer!
Tom Sawyer who?
Tom Saw-yer underwear!

What do you call underwear
with a picture of the night
sky on it?

Fruit of the moons!

What kind of underwear does a giant wear?

Long johns!

What do you put on under your dress when you want to sneak out of a movie early?

A slip!

What do you call your most brightly colored boxers?

Your fundies!

Knock, knock!
Who's there?
Pam!
Pam who?
Pam-per that baby so she doesn't wet herself!

What do you call three pairs of work socks?

A socket set!

What do you call boxer shorts with only one leg?

Blunderwear!

Why did everyone shun the dark underwear?

Because it was the black shorts of the family!

Why did the underwear want to sneak into the drawer unnoticed?

Because it didn't want any fanny-fare!

Why did the man put his underwear on before his striped pants?

He wanted to see it behind bars!

What do you call people who think about how the back of their underwear looks?

Hind-brained!

Why did the underwear want everyone to see him being active?

Because he didn't want people to think he was bum-bling!

What do you call it when you don't need to take your shorts to the cleaner?

Wash and underwear!

Knock, knock!
Who's there?
Underwear!
Underwear who?
Underwear my pants are!

What do you call your full-body Fruit of the Looms?

Your fruit suit!

Where do you wear the swimsuit that you've wanted to wear all year?

In the waiting pool!

What do you call the fast swimming style that your new bathing suit gives you?

A stroke of genius!

Where did the stylish new swimsuit put the racer?

In the fast lane!

Why did the cheap boxer shorts salesman do so well?

Because he under-cut the competition!

What kind of underwear do superheroines wear?

Wonderwear!

≋

Why did the underwear feel so low?

Because they just bottomed out!

≋

Knock, knock!
Who's there?
Owen!
Owen who?
I Owen 10 pairs of boxer shorts!

What do you call the most
helpful socks?

Support hose!

What kind of boxers will you
get for the holidays?

*Yule have to wait
to find out!*

What do you call formal
boxer shorts?

Butt-on downs!

What kind of movies do
underpants love?

Boxer short films!

How can you spot dancing
underwear?

With polka dots!

What do you call it when the lining of a dress gets tangled?

A slip knot!

What did the boxer shorts say to the airplane pilot's trousers?

You're flying awfully low, aren't you?

What kind of shorts do big cats wear?

Panther pants!

What do you call an underwear history book?

A brief history of time!

What do the writing instructions on a package of jockey shorts say?

Keep in pouch!

What do boxer shorts think of this book?

It's unbe-brief-able!

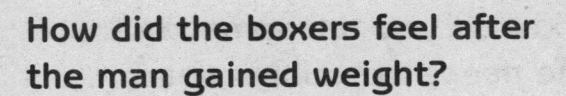

How did the boxers feel after the man gained weight?

Stretched to the limit!

What did the old man think of the idea of breathable shorts?

He really cott-on to the idea!

Knock, knock!
Who's there?
Enid!
Enid who?
Enid a clean pair of underwear!

How do you tell someone that he needs new underwear?

Briefly!

What is it called when you take off your shorts at night?

De-briefing!

What do you get when you put old underpants on an antenna?

A smelly telly!

What did the man say when his friend told him that his shorts had ripped right down the middle?

Seams that way, don't it?

Why did the boxer shorts feel betrayed?

They felt that they had been hung out to dry!

Why should you always wear underwear to bed?

In case you get woken up on short notice!

What do you call shorts that have lost their elastic?

Ex-spandex!

What do you call ancient dog underwear?

Old yeller!

What do felines wear to bed?

The cat's pajamas!

What did the canine say when her underwear ripped?

Doggone boxers!

What do apes who make boxer shorts call their shop?

Monkey business!

Why did the sailor want his underwear to ride low?

So that people could see his naval!

What do wolves think of boxer shorts jokes?

They think they're a howl!

What do owls think of boxer
shorts jokes?

They think they're a hoot!

What do you call it when
boxer shorts get caught on
a nail?

Under tear!

Knock, knock!
Who's there?
Sabrina!
Sabrina who?
*Sabrina long time since I've
changed my underwear!*

Was the man nervous about
how comfortable his new
boxer shorts would be?

Yes, he was a little weary!

What do you call tiny boxer
shorts for Teddy bears?

Bear-ly theres!

What do you call a shop
that sells boxers shorts in
the forest?

Bear-ly wares!

What do you call underwear made of wood?

Birch boxers!

What do artists wear on really hot days?

Just boxers and smocksers!

What do you call shorts with a back pocket?

A fanny pack!

What do you call the mama,
papa, and baby underwear
that live in the woods?

The three wears!

≈

What do you do say to
people who won't stop telling
underwear jokes?

*You tell them to
make it short!*

≈

What do you call someone
who wears frilly shorts?

Mr. Fancy Pants!

What do you call unattractive underwear that are too small?

Ugly snugglies!

What do you call a place where boxer shorts roam free?

The fanny farm!

What kind of card game do boxer shorts like to play?

Britch, of course!

Knock, knock!
Who's there?
Ice cream!
Ice cream who?
Ice creamed when my underpants fell down!

What do you call someone who steals your long underwear?

A woolly bully!

When is it bad to let someone put long johns on
your head?

**When he's trying to pull the
wool over your eyes!**

How do sheep feel about
woolen underwear?

Freezing!

What did one silk spinner say
to the other?

**Don't try to worm your
way out of this!**

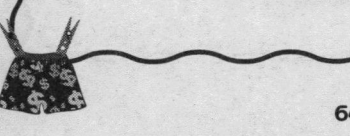

How did the farmer feel about taking away all the wool to make underwear?

A little sheepish!

≋

How did the farmer feel about his healthy herd for the underwear season?

He thought they were in sheep shape!

What did the sheep call their cross-country trip?

From Shorn to Shorn!

≈≈≈

What did the sheep think when it narrowly avoided having its wool taken to market?

That was a close shave!

≈≈≈

How did the farmer export his wares to the underwear shop?

He had them sheeped out!

What do you call the detergent you use to clean your boxer shorts?

Sham-poo!

≋

How did the sheep feel about the crazy farmer who took all their wool for underwear?

They thought it was shear madness!

≋

What did the man think about his cherry-patterned underwear?

He thought they looked short but sweet!

What do you call the boxer shorts that you wear at the beginning of the week?

Your Monday undies!

Why did the woman throw out her underwear?

Because they had become moldy oldies!

Where do long underwear go to dance?

The moth ball!

What did the one moth say
to the other when it saw the
long underwear?

Let's eat!

What do you call underwear
that you change into
at noon?

A boxered lunch!

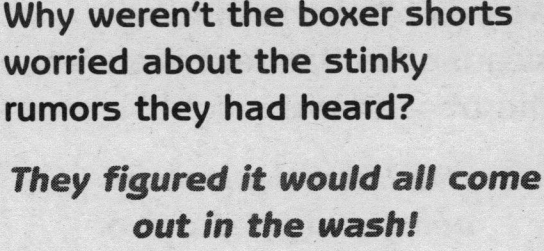

Why weren't the boxer shorts
worried about the stinky
rumors they had heard?

*They figured it would all come
out in the wash!*

≋

Why are old boxer shorts
worried about getting wet?

*Because they really have to
wash their figure!*

≋

Why were the boxer shorts so
proud of themselves?

*Because they were snug
and smug!*

Why didn't the man mind
wearing his flannel boxers on
the transatlantic flight?

*He liked the idea of
being snuggled out of
the country!*

Knock, knock!
Who's there?
India!
India who?
*India morning I always
change my underwear!*

Why did the man sit on the radiator in his boxers?

Because he wanted to toast his buns!

What do you think about boxer shorts for rabbits?

They're pretty bunny!

What did the boxer shorts say about being ignored?

Why do you treat me like a bum?

What did the silk underwear
say about the cotton
boxer shorts?

Pay them no hind!

Where do boxer shorts for
astronauts go?

To underspace!

How did the old boxer
shorts feel?

Under appreciated!

What did the old man say
about his favorite shorts?

I love my goody two shorts!

How did the woman feel about
her low-rise underwear?

*She thought they
were pretty hip!*

Why did the two legs of the long johns want to stay together?

They were an old couple!

≋

What did the man wear under his suit at the luncheon?

His tea shirt!

≋

Knock, knock!
Who's there?
Kenya!
Kenya who?
Kenya guess what color my underwear is?

What do you call someone
who loves to look for
underwear?

Short-sighted!

≋

How did the long johns know
they were going to be
shortened?

*They saw it coming at
the cut-off!*

≋

What do you call bright
silk briefs?

Shiny tinies!

What did the underwear call
the big, dim-witted man who
wore them?

A simple-ton!

What do you call boxers that
are too big?

Roomy bloomers!

Where is the best place to buy
boxer shorts?

Bloomer-dales, of course!

How did the captain feel about going down with the ship in his underwear?

He had a shrinking feeling!

What do you call shorts held up with ivory?

Waist-boned!

Why did the Neanderthal suddenly start wearing underwear?

One day, he just caved!

≈≈≈

What kind of shorts did dinosaurs wear?

Bronto boxers!

≈≈≈

How did the man feel about getting his shorts caught on the door handle?

He was a little hung up about it!

What do you call someone who wears camouflage boxers?

Under cover!

≋

Knock, knock!
Who's there?
Izzy!
Izzy who?
Izzy wearing any underwear?

≋

What do you call stockings that blow in the breeze?

Wind socks!

≋

What did the designer think
about her new line of hosiery?

*She thought it was a
big sock-sess!*

≋

What do you call a Scottish
stocking puppet?

The Sock-Ness monster!

≋

Why do you put wet shorts on
the line?

*So they'll be high
and dry!*

Why did the boxer shorts like being on the clothesline?

They just started to get the hang of it!

Why didn't the boxer shorts want to be put away?

Because they thought it would hamper their style!

What is it called when someone works out in his underwear?

Boxer-cize!

≈

What do you call all your favorite underwear when it's together for the first time?

A boxed set!

≈

Why did the socks feel so confident?

Because they knew they were a shoe-in!

How quickly did the young man put on his boxers?

In a zip!

What kind of insect lives in some underwear?

The button fly!

What do you call the peg where you hang up your underwear?

The butt-on!

How did the dress feel about the see-through tights?

Sheer delight!

Knock, knock!
Who's there?
Butter!
Butter who?
Butter make sure your underwear isn't showing!

How do you know when your underwear is tired?

When it can't stay up any longer!

What did the underwear button say to the hole?

The eyes have it!

What do you call a tricky fastener?

A tripper zipper!

How did the man know his shorts were unhappy?

They got themselves into a real flap!

What do you call long-haired underwear?

Hippies!

How many boxer shorts does it take to make a fruit salad?

Just one pear!

≋

What did they call the monster that ran around in its boxer shorts?

The under-were-wolf!

≋

Why do you feel so secure in your underwear?

Because you know they've got you covered!

≋

Why did the man think that his loose underwear was like a pizza?

Because he had to pick them up!

Why is the flap on boxer shorts so attentive?

It sits front and center!

≋

What do you call underwear that you can't decide whether or not to buy?

Iffy skivvies!

≋

Why is one sock always missing from the wash?

Because they just wander from the launder!

≋

What do you get when you forget to separate the dark colors from the bright, white boxer shorts?

Blue bottoms!

How do you know when it's getting late for your underwear?

When time is running shorts!

Knock, knock!
Who's there?
Harlow!
Harlow who?
Harlow do you wear your underpants?

What do you say when you see someone's underwear hanging out?

You look like you're waisting away!

What is the best way to get into the whole topic of underwear?

One foot at a time!

What did the man think about his new underwear's waistband?

He thought it was pretty snappy!

What did the man think about his unraveling underwear?

He thought that they had lost the thread somewhere!

Knock, Knock!
Who's there?
Abel!
Abel who?
I'm Abel to see your underwear!

What did the sock think about the stuffy underwear?

It thought that they were a little full of themselves!

Why was the underwear
so sad?

Because it was bummed out!

How do you feel when you put
on a new pair of boxers?

Short changed!

In what area does your
underwear like to hang out?

Near the rear!

Did it take long for the new underwear styles to become popular?

No, they really cott-on quickly!

Why should suspenders be arrested?

For holding up your shorts!

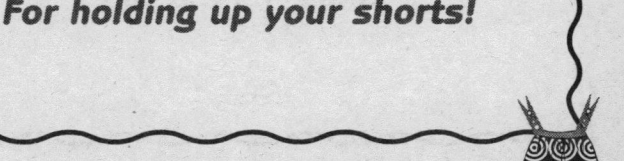

What do you call a playwright who goes on and on about stockings?

Sockspeare!

≈

Knock, knock!
Who's there?
Captain!
Captain who?
Captain Underpants!

≈

What kind of underwear did the big old elephant wear?

Woolly mammoths!

≈

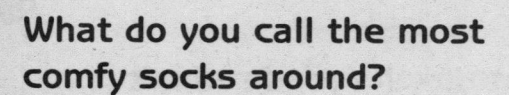

What do you call the most comfy socks around?

Cozy toesies!

≋

What did the boxer shorts say to the stockings that were hanging out to dry?

Oh, don't give me that old line!

≋

Knock, knock
Who's there!
Gertie!
Gertie who?
Gertie underwear goes in the hamper!

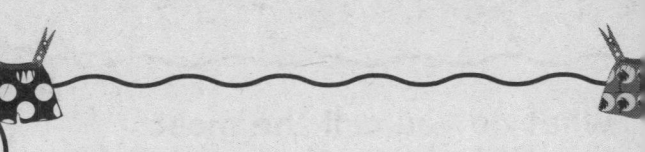

What did the reader think of the boxer shorts jokes?

They wore him out!

What do you say about a book like this one?

It's way too boxer short!